Longman Structural Readers
Stage 2

Double fear
and other stories

John Escott

Photographs by Lance Brown

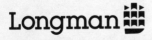

Longman Group Limited,
*Longman House, Burnt Mill, Harlow,
Essex CM20 2JE, England
Associated companies throughout the world.*

© Longman Group Limited 1983

*All rights reserved; no part of this publication
may be reproduced, stored in a retrieval system
or transmitted in any form or by any means, electronic,
mechanical, photocopying, recording, or otherwise,
without the prior written permission of the Publishers.*

First published 1983
Second impression 1985
ISBN 0 582 52786 4

Produced by Longman Singapore Publishers Pte Ltd.
Printed in Singapore.

Contents

	page
Double fear	1
Night music	25
The man from yesterday	35
Exercises	44

Double fear

The snow came to the south one day in January, and on that day Greg Mason saw his Double.

Greg was on his way home from work. At Hangar Hill he got off his bicycle and walked. The wind was in his face, and he had to push his bicycle up the hill through the snow.

"I don't often have to get off and push," he thought. "This snow makes hard work." He thought about the warm fire at home.

His head was down and he saw the other person's feet and legs first. It was a young man.

"Hello," the young man said. There was a smile on his face, but it was not a nice smile.

Greg looked at him through the snow. "He's wearing my shoes," he thought, "and my coat. But *I'm* wearing them. They can't be my things, but they're like them – just like them."

"Are you going home?" the other man asked.

Greg just nodded his head. "Why can't I answer?" he wondered. "He's just like me – my face, my hair, my eyes. But –"

The young man was *exactly* like Greg. He was Greg's exact double.

"You live in Hangar Lane," the Double said. It wasn't a question. The Double knew.

Greg nodded again. He hadn't any words. "Who is it?" he wondered. And suddenly his world was cold – not with the cold of the snow or the winter wind.

The Double smiled at Greg's surprised face. "Yes, Hangar Lane," he said. "It isn't near your place of work, is it?"

Greg spoke then. "You know me? You know my place of work? I don't understand."

"Don't be surprised," the Double said. "I know a lot about

1

you. I have to know a lot." He smiled again – not a kind smile. "I'll see you again – soon."

Then he walked down the hill.

Greg watched him. "Did it really happen?" he wondered. "Have I really got a double? And does he know all about me? Can I believe that?"

His mother gave him a cup of tea. "You're late tonight," she said. "Yes," Greg said. And he thought, "I can't tell her about the Double. What will she think? It's like a story in a book. Things like that don't really happen. People won't believe it."

Greg's father came in. There was snow on his shoes, and his face was red from the wind.

"What a night!" Mr Mason said. "The wind's very cold now."

He sat down at the table beside his son, and Mrs Mason brought him his tea. "Thank you," he said. Then he looked at Greg. "You were at work this afternoon, weren't you?" he said.

Greg was surprised. He said, "Yes, of course I was. Why do you ask?"

"I'm working in Kimble Street," Mr Mason said. He was a builder. "I saw a young man just like you in the street. His coat was like your coat, and he was like you in the face too."

"I wasn't in Kimble Street today," Greg said. And he thought, "Shall I tell them about the Double?" He wanted to tell them, but – "Why can't I speak about him? What's stopping me?" He didn't know. He just drank his tea and didn't speak.

His father liked the early evening news on television.

... And now the weather. There was some snow in the south of England today ...

"That's right," Mr Mason said. "There was a lot of snow."

Greg didn't hear him. His eyes were on the television.

2

There hasn't been any news of UFOs – unidentified flying objects or "flying saucers" – this week. People are wondering about last week's story of a UFO in the south of England.

"UFOs! Flying saucers!" Mr Mason said. "Things from outer space, with people from other worlds! You don't believe it, do you?"

"What was that, dear?" Mrs Mason asked.

"Don't you remember?" he said. "It happened last Saturday. Here, in this town. Some people saw a big thing in the sky. 'It's a flying saucer from outer space,' they said. One man told the television news people, 'It came down in a field on the north side of the town.'"

"Yes, I remember now," Mrs Mason said. "He took them to the field, and the flying saucer wasn't there."

"It was never there," Mr Mason said. "It was a dream."

"Was my Double a dream?" Greg wondered.

Greg did not sleep well. He dressed quickly in the morning and went down to the kitchen.

Mrs Mason was there. "It snowed again in the night," she said. "You'll be careful on the road, won't you? The snow's very deep."

Greg did not take his bicycle: he walked. But he stopped suddenly at the top of Hangar Hill.

The Double was at the bottom of the hill.

"So it's not a dream," Greg thought. "The Double is real."

He went down the hill. The Double smiled at him. He was exactly like Greg, but the smile was not kind.

"Who are you?" Greg asked. "Why are you here?"

The Double looked at him, and it was Greg's face. Then he began to speak. "Who am I? I am you – or I will be," he said. "Why am I here? Because you are here."

Greg did not speak. "What is happening?" he wondered. "There can't be another Greg Mason. I am Greg Mason."

"I'm waiting," the Double said. He was angry.

"Waiting for what?" Greg asked.

"Waiting to be you," the Double said. He moved nearer to Greg. "And I *will* be you. You won't always stop me."

Then the Double walked away.

Greg worked in an office and he sat near the window. Mike Wood sat next to him. Mike and Greg were friends.

Greg looked out at the car park. "It's snowing again this afternoon," he thought. The car park was white and the cars were white.

"Mike doesn't know about the Double yet," Greg thought. "I want to tell him, but I can't find the right words."

Mike looked at Greg and spoke. "*He* likes the snow," he said, and he pointed out of the window.

Greg looked out at the car park. He saw a man in the snow.

"Who is it?" Greg wondered. "I can't see his face."

"He's wearing your coat and scarf," Mike said.

"Yes," Greg said. "They *are* my things." He was suddenly cold.

"He's going now," Mike said. "Who is he, I wonder?"

Greg did not wonder. He knew. "It was him," he thought. "It was the Double. Why did he come? What does he want from me?"

Greg went home after work.

"Here he is," Mr Mason said. "You didn't see me this afternoon, Greg."

"This afternoon?" Greg said.

"Yes," Mr Mason said. "You were in Kimble Street. I saw you. You looked into a shop window – Mrs Harris's shop."

"It wasn't me," Greg said.

His father was angry. "It *was* you. I know my son, don't I?" he said. "What's wrong, Greg?"

"It wasn't me," Greg said. "It was another person."

Mr Mason smiled. "It was your double, was it?"

"That's right," Greg said quickly. "It was the Double."

His mother and father looked at him.

"*The* Double?" Mrs Mason said. "Greg, what are you talking about?"

"Don't tell lies, Greg," Mr Mason said. "I saw *you*. You looked into the shop window. Why were you in Kimble Street and not at work?"

Greg was angry. "I was not in Kimble Street! It wasn't me!" He looked at their surprised faces. They did not believe him.

"Your tea's on the table, Greg," Mrs Mason said softly.

"Thank you." Greg smiled at her. "I mustn't be angry," he thought. But he was afraid.

He went out after tea. On Fridays he always met Mike Wood at their club to play snooker. The club had four snooker tables.

"I mustn't be late," Greg thought. "Mike likes to get the best snooker table."

The Double was at the bottom of Hangar Hill again.

"You!" Greg said, but he was not surprised this time. "Who are you?"

"I am you," the Double told him.

"Stop it!" Greg said. "Don't say that again."

"But it's right; I *am* you" the Double said, "or I will be soon. I shall be real, like you. All of us will be real like our Earth Doubles."

"'Us?' What are you talking about?" Greg said. He was afraid again.

"I am not the only one," the Double said. "There are four others. But I am the only one of you. Or I *will* be you – I *will* make my Transfer!" He was angry again. "The others have made their Transfers. Why can't I make *my* Transfer? Why are you stopping me?"

"Transfer?" Greg said. "I don't understand."

"We are like two pictures," the Double said. "That's wrong. We must be one. It *must* happen."

Greg had to run away. He did not want this "Transfer"

thing to happen to him. He forgot about snooker at the club and about Mike. He ran and did not stop for a long time.

There were lights in the shop windows, but there were not many people in the streets. It was very cold.

Greg remembered the Double's words: "*All of us will be real like our Earth Doubles.*"

"Earth Doubles?" Greg thought. "So what is the Double? Where does it come from? Does it come from a place *not* on Earth?"

Suddenly, Greg remembered Mike. "Perhaps he knows the answer," he thought. "Oh! He's at the club – and he's wondering about me. Other people have got the best snooker table. Maybe Mike isn't waiting now."

Greg wanted to talk to Mike now. He wanted to tell Mike about the Double. "Maybe Mike can help me."

He ran all the way to the club. There were lights in the club rooms. Greg looked through a window and his eyes opened wide.

"Mike's there! He hasn't gone home. He's playing snooker, and he's playing on the best table!"

Then Greg saw the other man at the table with Mike. It was – the Double! Greg's Double!

Greg ran away from the window. "What's happening?" he thought. "Am *I* still the real Greg Mason?"

He ran and walked through dark streets between the houses. He walked across the park; the grass was white with snow. There were other people there, but he did not see them.

He was still cold and afraid. After a time, he found a cafe. "It'll be warm in there," he thought, "and I need a hot drink." So he opened the door.

He sat down at a table and a waitress came across the room.

"Do you want a cup of coffee?" the waitress asked Greg.

"Yes, please," Greg said.

There was one other person in the room. It was an old woman. She sat near the window but she did not look at Greg.

"Why can't I forget Mike and the Double?" he thought. "It wasn't the real Greg Mason. Didn't Mike know that?"

The waitress came back with the coffee.

"Thanks," Greg said.

There was an evening newspaper on the next table. Greg looked at it.

"WINTER WEATHER WON'T STOP YET" the front page of the paper said.

Greg took the paper and opened it up. He looked at an inside page.

"I REALLY SAW UFO," man says

People are still talking about last week's UFO. Our reporter spoke to Mr Arthur Trent. "It really was a UFO," Mr Trent told the reporter. "I saw it on Saturday night. It came down in a field. People have looked in the fields, I know. And they haven't found any footmarks or other marks – I know, I know! My wife and family don't believe me. A dream, they say. But *I* saw it, and *I* know. It was real – a real flying saucer. Not a dream."

Greg put the paper down on the table. UFOs. People from other worlds. It was strange.

Strange like the Double.

Suddenly, he saw a fire engine through the window. It was in a hurry.

Greg drank his coffee. "I must go home," he thought. "It's late."

The fire engine stopped at the end of the street. It was a long street, with a college at one end.

"It's the college." Greg thought. "The fire's there!"

He started to run. At the end of the street, he saw the fire engine in the college car park. There was an ambulance in the street, and a small crowd.

"What happened?" Greg asked a woman in the crowd. "How did the fire start?"

"Two students started it, perhaps," the woman said. "A

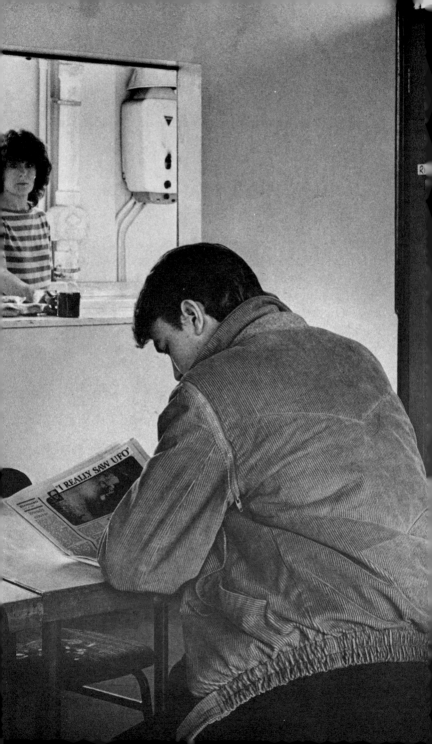

policeman told an ambulanceman that, and I heard."

Greg saw a police car behind the ambulance. "Two college students?" he said.

"Yes," the woman said. "The fireman found two bodies. They are in the ambulance now."

A man went into the back of the ambulance.

"That's the head of the college," the woman said.

"He knows all the students and he's going to look at the two bodies," said a man next to her.

After a minute, the college head came out of the ambulance. His face was white.

Greg didn't stay. He walked slowly back to Hangar Lane. Nearly all the houses were dark, but there was a light in Greg's house, and there was a car in the road near the front door.

It was a police car.

"There you are, Greg," Mr Mason said.

Greg looked at the two people with his father and mother. A policewoman was in a chair, and a policeman stood next to Mr Mason.

"Is this your son?" said the policeman.

"Yes," Mr Mason said.

The policeman walked across to Greg. "Where were you?" he asked.

"In the town," Greg said. "I walked through the streets. And I stopped to see the fire at the college."

"Fire?" Mrs Mason said. "Was there a fire at the college?"

"Yes," said the policewoman. "I heard it on the car radio. Two students started it, and they died in the fire."

"Oh, dear," Mrs Mason said. "But why did they do it?"

"We don't know," the policeman said. "They were two very good students; they never did things like that. But this evening they were like two different people."

The policewoman looked at Greg. "Where did you walk?" she asked.

"Greg –" his mother said.

"Just a minute," the policewoman told her. She turned back to Greg. "Where did you walk before the fire?"

"I – I don't know," Greg said. "I just walked. I went to a cafe."

"Did you go to Kimble Street before that?" the policewoman said.

"Kimble Street? No – or I don't think –"

"Don't you *know*?" the policewoman said.

"Well – no," Greg said.

"You *were* in Kimble Street," the policewoman told him. "You broke a shop window and took a clock."

"*What*? But I didn't!" Greg said. "It wasn't me. I wasn't there."

"It was Mrs Harris's shop, Greg," his father told him.

"And Mrs Harris saw you," the policewoman said. "She knows your face."

"Maybe Mrs Harris was wrong," Mr Mason said. "Maybe it was a different person."

"She saw Greg's face," the policeman said.

"Then where is the clock?" Greg said quickly. "I haven't got it. Look." He held up his arms.

The policeman looked at Mr Mason. "Perhaps he left it in another person's house on the way home," he said.

"What?" Greg said. "What did you say? I didn't hear you."

The policeman turned back to Greg. "You must come to the police station tomorrow afternoon," he said. "We'll speak to you again then."

The policewoman stood up. Mr Mason took them to the front door.

Greg wanted to shout after them, "It wasn't me. It was the Double. The Double took the clock." He wanted to shout this at them, but he didn't.

Mr Mason came back. "You were in Kimble Street this afternoon, Greg," he said. "But I didn't tell them that. It wasn't a good thing to say."

10

"I wasn't in Kimble Street today!" Greg shouted. "I've *told* you that!"

They looked at him, then his mother said, "You need some sleep, Greg. Go to bed."

Greg went up to his room. "Was I in Kimble Street tonight?"

Then he remembered the policeman's words about the two college students. The policeman said, "*They were like two different people.*"

And then Greg knew. They *were* two different people. *They were their own Doubles. Their* Doubles made the Transfer.

"... And now they're dead," Greg thought. "What did my Double say? 'There are four others.' That makes five Doubles with my Double. Now two are dead. Am *I* going to die next?"

"Something is happening. Is it a dream?"

There were faces. Faces like Greg's face. A lot of faces. Then just one face – his own face, but *not* his own face. Now the face was bigger – and bigger – and BIGGER.

"No – no!" Greg shouted. "Stop! Stop!"

Then another voice: "WHY? ... WHY? ... WHAT IS STOPPING ...?" it said.

"Stop!" Greg shouted again. "Who are you? What are you?"

"WHY?" the voice said again. "WHY CAN'T ... ?"

And then it stopped. Greg sat up in bed. "Was it a dream?" he thought.

His room was dark but he got out of bed and walked over to the window. He looked out. There was a moon in the sky and the ground was white. It was very quiet.

"What happened?" he thought. "Am I still me? Am I still Greg Mason? I am. I *must* be. But I know something: it was the Double. The Double tried to make the Transfer!"

It did not snow again that night, but the morning was cold. It was Saturday, and Greg did not go to work on Saturdays.

He went down to breakfast. His mother was already in the kitchen.

"Are you going out this morning?" she asked.

"Yes," he said. "I'm going to see Mike."

He wanted to tell Mike about the Double. He needed help, and maybe Mike knew the right thing to do.

"Don't forget to go to the police station this afternoon," his mother told him.

"I won't forget," he said.

There were not many people in the streets. It was very cold and they did not want to come out. There was ice on the road and the cars moved slowly. With ice on them, the roads were dangerous.

Suddenly, he saw a motorbike and his eyes opened wide. The motorbike came from the end of the street, and Greg saw the face of the rider.

"David!" he said. "David Blake!"

Greg lived near David Blake and knew him.

"What's he doing?" Greg wondered. "He's riding fast, and there's ice on the road. It's dangerous. He'll crash!"

The motorbike came up the street very fast. Suddenly, its back wheel slid to one side; motorbike and rider went down on the road with a crash.

"David!" Greg shouted.

A car came from the other end of the street. David and the motorbike were across the road in front of it. The driver of the car tried to stop, but his wheels slid on the ice, and there was another crash.

Greg ran along the street, and people came out of their houses at the noise.

David Blake lay on the icy road. He was dead.

A man came up beside Greg. He looked down at David. "Why did he do it?" he said. "Did you see the crash?"

"He went very fast on the icy road," Greg said. "But I don't understand; David hasn't got a motorbike."

"I know," the man said. "It's my motorbike. He took it from my house, I saw him."

"That's a lie!" Greg shouted. "David doesn't take things like that."

"He took my motorbike," the man said. "My wife saw him too. But he didn't know about motorbikes on icy roads."

The police came soon after. They were different policemen – Greg didn't know them. He told them about the crash, and they listened.

"He took my motorbike," the other man said. "I knew him. It wasn't like him to take my motorbike. He was like a different person. A different person with David's face."

"He *was* a different person," Greg thought. "Three of them are dead. Will there be another? Will it be me?"

The Double was at the end of Mike's street.

"It's you," Greg said.

"Yes," the Double said.

"Then I am still me," Greg thought.

"You won't stop me," the Double said. "I will make the Transfer. I *must*."

"You – you tried last night," Greg said.

"Yes," the Double said. "And I shall try again."

Greg looked at him for a minute – looked at his own face, his own body, his clothes, his shoes. It was very strange.

"Why did you take the clock from the shop?" Greg asked.

"I wanted it," the Double said. "Clocks are strange things. We don't have them in our place."

"Where is your place?" Greg asked.

"It doesn't matter now," the Double said. "We can't go back. We must stay here."

"Three of your – your friends are dead," Greg told him. "And so three other people are dead: David Blake and two college students." He was angry. "I saw David's crash. I *saw* it."

"Three dead," the Double said. "So there are two of us now. Then one of us must live. I must live. I must make my Transfer and live."

He walked away.

"Wait!" Greg called.

The Double stopped. "What do you want?" he asked.

"You must take back the clock," Greg said. "You must take it back to Mrs Harris's shop. Where is it?"

The Double put his hand under his coat and took out the clock. "It's here," he said.

"You must take it back, and people mustn't see you," Greg said.

"Why?" said the Double.

"The police know about it," Greg said. "Mrs Harris saw you. She saw your face – my face. She has told the police, 'Greg took it.' "

The Double put the clock in his coat pocket. "I'll take it back," he said. "It doesn't matter. I don't want it now."

Greg turned and walked away.

Mike's mother came to open the door. "Hello, Greg," she said. "Do you want to see Mike?"

"Yes, please," Greg said.

"He's in his room," she said.

Greg went up the stairs.

Mike was in his room by the window. "Hello, Greg," he said. "Sit down."

Greg sat on the bed.

"That was a good game last night," Mike said.

"What game?" Greg asked.

Mike smiled. "The game of snooker," he said. "But you didn't play very well, did you?"

"Didn't I?" Greg said.

"No," Mike said. "You didn't play your best game. At other times you play a better game of snooker."

Then Greg said, "It wasn't me, Mike."

Mike's smile left his face. "What are you talking about?" he said.

"It wasn't me," Greg said again. "It was another person – a person just like me."

"I don't understand," Mike said.

"Do you know David Blake?" Greg asked.

"David? Yes, I know him," Mike said. "Why?"

"He's dead," Greg said.

"Dead!" Mike said.

Greg told him about the motorbike crash.

"But – but David never took another person's things," Mike said.

"It wasn't David," Greg said. "It was a person *like* David."

"Then who died?" Mike said. "What are you saying, Greg?"

"David is dead," Greg said. "His Double made the Transfer, so he's dead."

"Double? Transfer?" Mike said. "Greg, what are you talking about?"

"I'll tell you," Greg said. And he told Mike about his own Double, and about the students in the fire. He told him about the UFO.

"Why are you telling me about UFOs?" Mike asked.

"I don't really know," Greg said. "But maybe the Doubles came from the UFO."

They were quiet for a minute. Then Mike said, "Have you told any other person about this?"

"No," Greg said. "What can I do, Mike?"

Mike said, "You saw your Double. I wonder: did David see his Double? Or did David's Double make the Transfer and David didn't know?"

"I wonder," Greg said.

"Maybe the Double made the Transfer and David didn't know," Mike said. "Perhaps the students' Doubles did that too."

"Then why didn't my Double do that?" Greg said.

15

"I don't understand that," Mike said. "Maybe he can't. Maybe he wants to make the Transfer but he can't."

Greg remembered the voice from last night: "WHY? ... WHY? ... WHAT IS STOPPING ...?"

"Perhaps you're right," he told Mike.

"Then *what* is stopping him?" Mike said. "I want to see this Double."

"You saw him last night," Greg said.

"But I didn't know that then," Mike said. "Where is he now?"

"Maybe he's taking the clock back," Greg said.

"What clock?" Mike wanted to know.

Greg told him. Then he said, "We can go to the shop and see, but I don't want to go in."

"I'll go into the shop," Mike said. "You can wait at the end of the street."

"All right," Greg said.

Kimble Street was nearly empty. There were two women on a corner. A young man walked down the street with a black and white dog.

Greg and Mike stopped at the end of the street.

"I can't see the Double," Greg said.

"Maybe he'll come soon," Mike said. "Or maybe he has been here already."

The young man with the black and white dog came near to Greg and Mike.

"It's Bill Harper," Mike said. Both Greg and Mike knew the young man.

"Hello, Bill," Greg said.

"Hello, Bill," Mike said. He went to touch the dog.

"Leave him," Bill Harper said. "Don't touch him."

Mike was surprised. "It's only me, Bill," he said. "I only wanted to say hello to your dog."

The young man looked at Mike and Greg. He did not smile or speak. Then he walked on and the dog ran after him.

"Do you think . . . ?" Greg started.

"I don't know," Mike said. He was not happy. "He's just *like* Bill Harper."

Bill Harper, or the person *like* Bill Harper, went round the corner.

"I'll go to Mrs Harris's shop," Mike said then.

"I'll wait here," Greg said.

It was a small shop and it was full of old things. Mrs Harris was an old lady with white hair.

"Hello, Mrs Harris," Mike said.

"Hello, Mike," she said. "Are you going to buy something?"

"Er – a book," Mike said. "I'll look at those over there."

He went across to the corner of the room. There was a broken window at the side of the shop. A piece of wood was over the hole in the glass.

"The weather's bad," Mrs Harris said.

"Yes," Mike said. "We had a cold night."

"Yes, we did. I didn't sleep," she said.

"Why not?" Mike asked.

"The police came," she said.

"What did the police want," Mike said.

"They came about a clock. Greg Mason took a clock from my window," she said.

"Greg Mason took a clock?" Mike said. "I can't believe it."

"I saw him," Mrs Harris said. "He broke the side window, then put his hand in and took the clock. I saw his face."

"But why did Greg take a clock?" Mike said.

"I don't know," Mrs Harris said. "But he brought it back this morning."

"Did he?" Mike said. "Did you see him?"

"No, but he took it," she said, "so he brought it back."

"When was this?" Mike said.

"About eleven o'clock," Mrs Harris said. "I went up to

make a cup of coffee. Then I came down, and the clock was on that table. Look, it's still there."

There was a small table on the other side of the room, and Mike saw the clock on it.

"Well, Greg didn't bring it back, Mrs Harris," he said. "Greg was with me at that time. My mother will tell you that, too. She saw him. He came to our house at ten o'clock."

Mrs Harris was surprised. "But — but I don't understand."

"Maybe Greg didn't take the clock, Mrs Harris," Mike said. "Maybe you were wrong."

Mrs Harris thought for a minute. Then she said, "It was a dark night. Perhaps I was wrong. Perhaps the man was *like* Greg. Oh dear!"

"Well, you have your clock back," Mike said.

"Yes," Mrs Harris said. "I must telephone the police. Perhaps I was wrong. I must tell them."

"That's the best thing to do," Mike said. He took a book over to her. "Can I have this one?"

Mrs Harris looked at the book. "It's a book about UFOs," she said. "You don't believe in those things, do you?"

"I don't know, Mrs Harris," Mike said. "I don't know."

"What happened?" Greg wanted to know.

Mike told him. "She's going to telephone the police," he said. "The clock is back. She said, 'Perhaps I was wrong.'"

"Thanks, Mike," Greg said. "Thanks for your help."

They walked away from Kimble Street.

"I want to see your Double," Mike said.

"He doesn't speak to me with other people," Greg said.

Mike thought about that. "All right," he said. "I won't be with you. He won't see me, but I'll be very near."

They went to the park. Greg sat on a seat in an empty corner near some bushes. Mike went behind some bushes.

Greg sat on the seat and waited. "I wasn't really afraid

before," he thought. "But I'm afraid now." He watched some children; they played quietly in the snow. Slowly, very slowly, sleep came to him...

"IT MUST HAPPEN..." the voice said in his head. "IT MUST... IT MUST..."

Greg's head was full of the sound of the voice.

"WHY?... WHY?... WHAT IS STOPPING...?"

Greg put his hands over his face. "Stop! Stop!" he shouted.

The voice was angry. "NOW... NOW..." it said.

Slowly, the voice grew quieter.

Greg took his hands from his face and opened his eyes.

The Double was in front of him – very angry.

"What are you doing?" the Double said. "What are you doing to stop me? I *must* make the Transfer! You must tell me!"

"I – I don't know," Greg said.

The Double turned and started to walk away. Greg put his head in his hands and looked at the snow. He was sick and very tired.

The Double shouted back, "What's wrong? I *will* know. I *will* make the Transfer! I will know *today*!"

Greg did not hear him.

Mike came out from behind the bushes.

Greg looked up. "Did you see him?" he asked.

"Yes," Mike said quietly. "I still can't believe it."

Greg stood up and they walked along the path.

"We'll go down to the lake," Mike said. "It won't be very cold down there; the wind won't be very strong."

They went down the hill and between some tall trees. The lake was on the other side of the trees.

"The Double tried to make the Transfer," Greg said.

"Yes," Mike said. "I heard your shouts and I nearly came to help. Then you stopped, and there, suddenly, was the Double. I watched the two of you after that. It was very strange."

The lake was in front of them. It was very wide. There was thin ice on top of the water.

"Look," Mike said. "There's Bill Harper again."

Greg looked and saw the other young man. Bill Harper walked along the path. The black and white dog ran in front of him.

"What's he doing?" Greg said. "Look!"

Bill Harper walked off the path. Then he walked on to the thin ice on the lake.

"Stop!" Mike shouted. "Stop, or you'll go through the ice into the water!"

Perhaps Bill Harper did not hear. He walked on. He was on the ice and it started to break. Mike heard it. Crack! The black and white dog tried to pull him back. Greg and Mike ran along the path.

"Wait! Stop!" Greg shouted.

But Bill Harper did not stop. Suddenly, he went down through the ice and into the water.

Other people ran along the path. They were on the other side of the lake.

Bill Harper's head came up to the top three times. Then it went down and did not come up again.

They stood beside the lake – Greg, Mike and some other people. A police car was beside the trees. There were some policemen out in a boat, and one was in the water.

"Will they find him?" Greg asked Mike.

"I don't know," Mike said.

They were very cold. After the accident they stayed at the lake for nearly an hour. They told a policewoman about Bill Harper and the accident. A man and a woman told their story too.

"Why didn't he know about thin ice?" the woman said. "He walked on. The ice started to break, but he didn't stop. We shouted to him, and those young men shouted to him, but he still walked on. Didn't he know about ice?"

There was a shout from the boat.

"They've found him," the policewoman said. "I'll radio for an ambulance."

Greg walked away. He did not want to see another ambulance.

Mike and Greg left the park.

"My Double is the only one now," Greg said.

"Yes," Mike said. "I know."

"They don't understand things," Greg said. "They know some things but not others."

"Yes," Mike said. "And they die. Why do they die? *Because* they don't know. They didn't know about ice. They didn't know about fire. They didn't know about a motorbike in the snow."

"So they die," Greg said, "and the real people die with them. I – I don't want to die."

"We must stop your Double," Mike said.

"But how?" Greg said.

"I don't know," Mike said. "But we must do it quickly. You heard the Double's words."

"Which words?" Greg asked.

"You remember. He said, 'What's wrong? I *will* know. I *will* make the Transfer! I will know *today*!'"

Greg was surprised. "When did he say that?" he asked.

"This morning, in the park," Mike said. "You heard–" He stopped. His eyes opened wide. "*Now* I know," he said.

"What are you talking about, Mike?" Greg said.

"Why the Double can't make the Transfer," Mike said. "I know now."

"Why?" Greg asked. "Tell me!"

"He knows a lot about you, but he doesn't know *one* thing about you," Mike said. "He isn't *exactly* like you, and so he can't make the Transfer."

"What doesn't he know about me?" Greg asked.

Mike looked at Greg. He always looked at Greg to speak to

21

him. Greg looked at Mike. He always looked at other people's faces to understand them.

"You're deaf," Mike said. "You're different from us: you can't hear. You have to see a person's face, and *then* you can understand them. The Double doesn't know that."

Greg did not speak for a minute. Then he said, "Yes, you're right. But why did you say, 'I know now'?"

"I remember the seat in the park," Mike said. "The Double left you there and walked away. He shouted those words at you . . . *but he did not turn round*. He didn't turn, and so you didn't see his face. You are deaf, and he doesn't know it."

"BUT I KNOW NOW," the Double's voice said in Greg's head. "I KNOW NOW, AND I KNOW THE BEST THING TO DO . . ."

Greg put his hands to his head. "Stop! Stop!" he shouted.

Greg went home. Mike went to his own house.

"I'll see you tomorrow, Greg," Mike said. "I'll try to think and find an answer."

"Is there an answer?" Greg wondered.

At home, his mother said, "The police phoned."

"What did they say?" Greg asked.

"It's all right," she said. "Mrs Harris phoned them. She has the clock back. She told them, 'Perhaps I was wrong. Perhaps it wasn't Greg.'"

"She *was* wrong," Greg said. "But perhaps it doesn't matter now."

He did not sleep that night. He sat and waited. "The Double will try to make the Transfer tonight," he thought.

But the Double did not come.

In the morning he went to meet Mike. The snow lay on the ground, but the sun shone.

Mike was in the garden, near the front door of his house. "He's doing some work on his bike," Greg thought. And he said, "Hello, Mike."

Mike looked up. He didn't speak, and he didn't smile.

"I didn't sleep," Greg said. "Did you sleep all right?"

"Yes," Mike said. He was surprised at Greg's question.

"Nothing happened," Greg said. "The Double didn't try to make the Transfer."

Mike did not speak.

"Did you hear me, Mike?" Greg said. "What's the matter?"

"Nothing's the matter," Mike said. His voice was angry. "Why did you come? What do you want?"

Greg did not understand. "What's wrong?" he wondered. He said, "Don't you remember?" Then he stopped, and suddenly he was cold.

Mike looked at him. "What's the matter with you?" he said. His voice was still angry.

Greg did not speak.

"You can forget the Double," Mike told him. "You'll be all right. He won't want to make the Transfer with you. You're deaf, so he'll want to be another person."

"Will he?" Greg said softly.

"Yes," Mike said. "He will." Then he smiled. It was not a nice smile.

But Greg knew Mike's smile. This person was not Mike.

Night music

Cathy lived and worked in the city. She had a small car, and she drove it to her office every day.

"I'll drive into the country for my holiday in July," Cathy thought. "I'll take my camping things, and I'll stop at good country camping places."

In July, Cathy drove her car into the country. The sky was blue, the trees and the grass were green. The air was good. It was very different from the city. She drove on and on.

"What a beautiful day!" Cathy thought. "What a beautiful holiday! But I must find a camping place soon. I must put my tent up in the daylight."

She found a field behind an old church, and she put her tent up there. She took her sleeping bag out of the car.

"I'll sleep well tonight," she thought.

But she did not sleep well. She woke in the middle of the night.

"What is that sound?" she wondered. "I can hear music. Organ music."

Cathy got out of her sleeping bag and went out of the tent. There was a moon in the sky. She could see the old church across the field.

"The music's coming from there," she thought. "Who is playing the church organ in the middle of the night?"

Cathy walked over the field to the church. It had a high tower, and part of the tower was broken.

"I'm not afraid," she thought, "but the music *is* very loud, and the church is very old."

She pushed the big church door, and it opened.

The music stopped.

The light from the moon lit up the church, and she saw the organ. But there was nobody there. There was nobody at the organ – nobody in the church.

"I don't understand," she thought.

She walked back across the field. She did not sleep again that night.

Cathy got up very early and looked across to the church.

"Did I *really* hear music in the night?" she wondered. "Or was it a dream?"

The church stood on a hill. At the bottom of the hill, there were the houses and shops of a small village. Cathy went down to the village. It was very quiet, but one shop was open.

"I need some milk," Cathy thought. "Perhaps I can buy it here."

She went into the shop.

"Good morning," said the woman in the shop. "You're up early."

"I'm camping," Cathy told her. "I – I woke up early."

"What can I sell you?" the woman asked.

"Some milk, please," Cathy said. Then she went on: "You have a nice church."

The woman gave Cathy a strange look. "Have you been *in* the church?" she asked. "The door is nearly always locked."

"It wasn't locked last night," Cathy said.

"Last night?" the woman said. "Why did you go to the church last night?"

"I heard organ music in the middle of the night," Cathy answered.

The woman gave her another strange look. "The church organ is broken," she said. "Nobody can play it."

"Oh!" Cathy said. "Perhaps it was a dream."

The woman nodded. "A dream, yes," she said. "You had a dream."

"Why is she smiling now?" Cathy wondered.

Cathy came out into the street with her milk. She walked back up the hill.

She went to the church door, but it was locked.

"What do you want?" a voice said behind her.

Cathy turned. An old man stood behind her.

"Who are you?" she asked.

"Albert Purley," the man said. "I look after the church. The door's locked. People took things from the church, so the door's always locked now."

"It wasn't locked last night," Cathy said.

Purley gave Cathy a strange look. "Why do you say that?" he asked.

"Because I came here. I – I heard organ music. It was loud music, and it woke me. I came across to the church. The door wasn't locked, but the church was empty. Then the music stopped."

Purley did not speak for a minute.

"But he isn't surprised," Cathy thought.

In the end he said, "Is that your tent in the field?"

"Yes," Cathy said. "I'm on holiday."

"Are you going to stay here?" Purley asked.

"I don't know."

Purley nodded, but he did not speak again. After a minute, he walked away.

"He looks after the church, but he didn't tell me about the broken organ," Cathy thought. "I wonder why." Then she went back to her tent.

The day was hot. Cathy walked along the narrow roads and through the fields. People smiled and said, "Good morning." In the evening she sat beside her tent.

"I like it here," she thought. "It's beautiful and quiet."

She did not think about the organ music or the strange old church with the locked door. She did not *want* to think about them.

But in the middle of the night, Cathy woke up again. The world was quiet. And then she heard the organ music again.

For a long time, she just listened. She did not want to get out of her sleeping bag. She did not want to go to the church.

"But who is it?" she wondered. "I *must* know."

She went across the field to the church door. The music was very loud. "Can't they hear this in the village?" she thought.

The door was not locked. Cathy opened it. Again the light from the moon lit up the church. And the music stopped suddenly.

"I can see the organ," Cathy thought. "I can see – oh!"

There was a young man at the organ. He was on the organ seat, and his hands were on the organ. Suddenly he turned, and Cathy saw his face.

"Who –?" Cathy started to say.

But the young man was not there.

"He's gone!" Cathy said. "He *was* there, wasn't he? Or was he a dream too?"

She looked, but the church was empty. She went out again and shut the door. She started to walk away, but then she went back and tried to open the door.

"It's locked!" she said.

She ran back to her tent.

The next morning, the old man was near the church again. Cathy met him on her way back from the village.

"Good morning, Mr Purley," she said.

"Good morning," Purley said after a minute.

"Who *is* the young man at the organ?" Cathy asked.

"Young man? What young man?" Purley said. But he did not look at Cathy.

"He has black hair," Cathy said, "and he wears a black suit."

Purley looked at her. His face was white.

"He's afraid," Cathy thought.

"What do you know about him?" Purley wanted to know. "What do you know about Mr Heine?"

"Is that his name?" Cathy said. "Does he play the organ?"

"He *did* play it," Purley said. "Seventy years ago."

"Where is he now?" Cathy asked.

"Now? He's dead now. He died seventy years ago. He died after the wedding."

"What wedding?" Cathy wanted to know.

"The wedding of a girl in the village," Purley said. "The girl wanted to marry Mr Heine. She wanted to be his wife. But her father said, 'No, you will *not* marry Heine. Never!' And she had to marry another man. She did not love the other man, but she had to marry him."

"Did Mr Heine play the organ at the wedding?" Cathy asked.

"Yes. And after the wedding, he died."

Cathy thought about the young man at the organ. "Was that the dead Mr Heine?" she wondered. "Was it Mr Heine's *ghost*?" And she asked: "Have you heard the music, Mr Purley?"

"Yes," Purley said. "Other people in the village have heard it too."

"Why does his ghost come back and play the organ?" Cathy asked.

"I – I don't know," the old man said. "Perhaps he's playing for the girl. Perhaps he wants her to come to him."

"But isn't she dead now – after seventy years?" Cathy said. "Or very old?"

"She's dead," Purley said quietly. "She died a month after the wedding. She died in an accident at sea."

"But Mr Heine still plays for her," Cathy said in a sad voice. "So she didn't go to him after the accident. She died, but she didn't go to him."

"No," Purley said. After a minute, he went on: "When did you see Mr Heine?"

"Last night," Cathy said. "He was in the church."

Purley did not speak for a long time. He looked at Cathy's face and looked away – again and again. In the end, he said, "You must go away from here. Don't stay."

"Why?" Cathy asked.

"I don't know," he said. "I just know this: you mustn't stay. This place is dangerous for you."

And then he walked away.

"*Shall* I go?" Cathy wondered. "Maybe he's right. Ghosts *are* dangerous. But I want to stay. I want to know about this ghost at the organ."

The afternoon was very hot. The sun went in, and the sky was dark. Cathy looked at the large black clouds. "There's rain in those clouds," she thought. "Maybe there will be a thunderstorm."

Cathy did not like thunderstorms. She did not like the sudden flashes of lightning. She did not like the crash of thunder.

She stayed in her tent. There was some thunder, but it was not near yet. Night came, and she got into her sleeping bag. Soon after, the rain started.

"I don't like this," Cathy thought. "This rain's heavy, and it'll come into my tent. I'll go and sleep in the car."

She got out of her sleeping bag. Then she took down the tent, and she carried it and all her camping things to the car. In the heavy rain she was soon very wet. There was a sudden crash of thunder.

And there was another sound, over the noise of the thunder. It was organ music – and it came from the church.

Cathy stopped and listened. "I must go to the church," she thought. "*I have to go*."

She turned and walked across the wet field through the rain.

Purley lived in a small house in the village. He lived alone.

"I've lived alone for seventy years," he thought. "This year I'll be eighty-nine years old."

He thought about the girl with the tent. "It's a bad thunderstorm," he thought. "She'll get very wet." Then he thought about the church and the organ music – and he was afraid.

The thunderstorm went on. Crashes of thunder. Flashes of lightning. Purley listened – and he remembered another storm, years ago. A young man died in that storm. Lightning hit the church tower, and the young man died.

Then he heard the organ music. The sound of it came over the noise of the storm – over the crash of thunder. The music filled his small house.

"I must go up to the church," he thought. "The girl must not die."

Cathy walked to the church. Lightning flashed in the sky. It lit up the dark building and the tall broken tower. She walked like a person in a dream.

Purley came up the hill and saw her near the church.

"Stop!" he shouted. "Move away from the church!"

There was another flash of lightning. Cathy looked up at the top of the church tower. There was a face there.

"Mr Heine?" she called. "Is that you, Mr Heine?"

"Wait!" shouted Purley. "Stop!"

Mr Heine smiled at Cathy. He nodded and smiled again.

"Leave her! Leave her, Heine!" shouted Purley. "It's not her! Not her!"

Another flash of lightning – and this time it hit the tower. There was a crash, and some of the tower broke away and began to fall. It was going to fall on Cathy.

She tried to run. Her feet did not move. Then hands – an old man's hands – pushed her away. It was Purley.

They walked back to Purley's house. The storm was quieter. The dark church was behind them.

"Why – why did you come up to the church?" Cathy asked. It was still like a dream to her.

"It was the storm," Purley said. "I remembered Heine. He died in a storm just like this."

"What happened to him?" Cathy asked.

"Lightning hit the church tower, and a part of it came down. It fell on Heine and killed him. It was only two nights after the wedding."

"And I nearly died like that," Cathy said. "He tried to *kill me* like that?"

"Yes," Purley said.

"Why?"

"Because he loved the girl at the wedding," Purley told her. "To him, you were that girl. You – you are exactly like her. Your face is exactly like her face."

Cathy stopped. She turned to Purley. "I'm exactly like her?" she said. "How do you know that?"

"She married another man," Purley said quietly. "You remember that? I was that other man."

Much later, Cathy went back to her car. "I'm going to leave this place now," she thought. "I'm not going to wait for daylight. I'm going now."

The sound of organ music came across the fields.

Cathy put her hands over her ears.

The man from yesterday

It was a cold night in February in the north of England. There was snow on the motorway. Sam was a good driver, but he was tired.

"I must leave the motorway and find a hotel," Sam thought.

He left the motorway at the next exit, and he was soon in country lanes. There was snow on the ground and on all the trees and bushes. Sam drove slowly up a lane between tall trees. The snow was deep in the lane, and Sam wondered, "Was I wrong to leave the motorway?"

And then he saw the hotel – the *Woodlands Hotel*.

"Good," Sam thought. "I can stay here for the night."

He couldn't drive to the door of the hotel: there was a lot of snow there. He left his car under some trees.

"It's a very old hotel," he thought. He took his bag from his car and walked to the door.

It was not really warm in the hotel. Sam saw an old man behind a desk near the entrance.

"Can I help you?" the old man asked.

"Yes," Sam answered. "I'd like a room for the night, please."

The old man nodded. He opened a book on the desk top.

"Please sign the visitors' book," he said.

Sam signed the visitors' book: *Sam Craven*. He wrote the date, too: *1 February*.

"I'd like a meal soon," he said.

The old man gave Sam a key. "Room number 9," he said, "at the top of the stairs. They'll give you dinner in the dining room." And he pointed to the dining room door.

"Thank you," Sam said. He took his bag up to his room. It was a small, dark room. The bed and all the other things in the room were very old-fashioned.

He went down to the dining room. There were two women at a table near the door.

"Good evening," Sam said.

They looked at him and smiled. But there was a question in their smiles. Their eyes were on his clothes, and Sam looked at *their* clothes.

"My mother wore clothes like that," he thought "forty years ago."

There was a fireplace in a corner of the dining room, with a good fire in it. Sam sat down at a table near the fireplace. "Perhaps I'll be warm here," he thought. "It isn't a warm hotel."

A young man in waiter's clothes came into the room. His hair was black, and he had a black moustache – an old-fashioned moustache.

"Good evening, sir," he said to Sam. "Would you like dinner?"

"I'd like some hot soup," Sam said. "It's a cold night."

"Yes, sir," the waiter said. "Have you come a long way?"

"From Bristol. I turned off the motorway. There's a lot of snow on the roads, and the motorway is dangerous."

"The motorway?" It was a question.

"Yes," Sam said. "You know the motorway, don't you?"

For a minute the waiter didn't answer. Then he said: "I'll get your soup, sir."

"What a strange man!" Sam thought.

Sam went into the lounge after his meal. There was another fireplace, with another large fire in it. Sam sat down in a chair near the fire. There was a table beside his chair, with a magazine on it.

"Good," Sam thought. "I'll read a story in this magazine, and then I'll go to bed."

He opened the magazine and turned the pages.

"This is strange," he thought. "All the stories are about a

different time." He looked at the date on the front of the magazine: February 1947.

"It's more than thirty-five years old!" he thought.

He looked across the lounge. There were some magazines on another table near the door. Sam walked across the room and looked at them: December 1946, January 1947, February 1947!

Sam went up to his room. "This hotel needs some new magazines," he thought with a smile.

He did not sleep well. His room was cold. He got up early and went down to the dining room.

"Would you like some breakfast?" the waiter asked.

"Thank you," Sam said.

He ate his breakfast. Then he went to the old man at the desk and said, "I work for the Bristol Aircraft Company. Look, here's my card. Please send my hotel bill to the company."

The old man looked at the card: *The Bristol Aircraft Company – Sam Craven.* "Of course, sir. Will you just sign the bill here, please?"

Sam didn't really look at the bill. He just wrote his name on it. Then he carried his bag out and walked through the snow to his car. He looked back at the hotel.

"I won't stay at that old-fashioned place again," he thought.

In March, Sam's work in the north ended. He started his journey back to Bristol late in the evening. It was dark, and Sam was tired.

"I'll stop at a hotel," he thought, "and I'll finish my journey tomorrow."

He left the motorway at the next exit.

"I'm near the Woodlands Hotel," he remembered with a smile. "But I won't stay there. I'll find a newer hotel."

He found a newer hotel. It, too, was up a country lane. But the place was larger, and there was a car park at the front.

Sam parked his car and walked to the front doors. At the entrance, he looked at the name of the hotel. It was the *Woodlands Hotel*. He was surprised.

"Another hotel with that name!" he thought. "But this one's different. It's bigger and newer."

There was a desk near the entrance. A young woman sat behind it.

"Good evening, sir," she said. "Would you like a room, or have you only come for a meal?"

"I'd like a room, and I'd like dinner, too."

The girl rang a bell on the desk top. A man came from the room behind.

"George," the girl said, "take this gentleman's case up to room nine. Then the gentleman can go into the dining room for dinner."

George smiled at Sam and took his case.

"Will you sign the visitors' book, please?" the girl said.

Sam signed the book. Then he went into the dining room. It was not unlike the dining room in the other Woodlands Hotel, but it was larger and warmer. There were a lot of people in it. Sam found an empty table and sat down.

"Good evening, sir," a voice behind him said. "Would you like the menu?"

Sam turned quickly. It was the waiter from the other Woodlands Hotel. Or he was *like* the waiter from the other hotel. He had black hair – but he did not have a moustache.

Sam took the menu. "I – I'd like some soup," he said.

"Yes, sir," the waiter said.

"Haven't I seen you before?" Sam asked. "Didn't you work at another Woodlands Hotel near here?"

The man was surprised. He gave Sam a strange look.

"Does he remember me?" Sam wondered.

The waiter said, "There isn't another Woodlands Hotel near here, sir." Then he walked away.

The meal was very good. After it, Sam went into the hotel

lounge. There were magazines and papers in the lounge, and he looked at them.

"Well, these aren't thirty-five years old," he thought.

He slept well that night. The bed and his room were warm.

In the morning, early, he went down to the dining room. There were some pictures on the wall, and he looked at them.

He stopped at one picture and looked at it carefully. He was surprised. It was a picture of the other Woodlands Hotel.

There was nobody in the dining room, so Sam went out to the woman at the desk.

"Can you come into the dining room for a minute?" he said.

The woman was surprised, but she said, "All right."

He showed her the picture. "This is a picture of the other Woodlands Hotel, isn't it?"

"That's right," she said. "I never saw it, of course. But my father remembers it. He was a boy then."

"Your father was a boy! I don't understand."

The woman looked at him. "Oh, of course, you don't know," she said. "The old Woodlands Hotel burnt down thirty-five years ago. All the people in the hotel died in the fire. It happened in February 1947 – 10 February, 1947."

"1947?" Sam said.

The young woman nodded. "They built this hotel in the same place," she said. "So they gave it the same name: the Woodlands Hotel."

Sam looked at the picture, and he wondered: "Is this right? But I *stayed* at that hotel! Last month! Didn't I?" And he asked the woman, "Didn't they save anybody?"

"Nobody, my father says. They did save some *things* – some books and things. We still have the old visitors' book."

Sam turned quickly. "Can I see the visitors' book?" he asked.

The woman was surprised. "Er – yes," she said. "Yes, of course."

They went back to the desk, and the young woman went

into the room at the back. She came out with a book and put it on the desk.

There were marks of the fire on it, but Sam knew it. He turned the pages.

It was there!

Sam Craven – 1 February.

He looked at the date at the top of the page: *1947.*

"I didn't look there before," he thought.

He shut the book and gave it back to the woman. "Thank you," he said.

She nodded to the dining room. "Would you like breakfast now?" she asked. "Roger is there."

"Roger?" Sam said.

"The waiter."

Sam turned and saw the waiter in the dining room. "Has he been at this hotel for a long time?" he asked the woman.

"Er – yes," she said. "But nobody knows much about him. He's a strange man."

"Strange?"

"Yes, sir. He just arrived one day. He's a young man, but he's a very good waiter. He knows his job like an older man, but he's not old."

"Does he live in the hotel?" Sam asked.

"Yes. He goes away for a holiday every year – at a strange time of year for a holiday. In February."

"February?"

"Yes. Every year."

Sam didn't speak for a minute. Then he said, "The fire in the old hotel – where did it start?"

"In a room at the back – they say. A waiter's room. 'Perhaps he fell asleep with a cigarette,' my father says. 'Nobody really knows, and the waiter died in the fire. But that's the story.' "

Sam went into the dining room.

"Good morning, sir," the waiter said.

"Good morning, Roger," Sam answered.

"Would you like breakfast, sir?"

"Yes, please," Sam said. The waiter moved away, and Sam watched him.

Sam sat and thought. "What happened to me last month? A very strange thing. I stepped back into another time. I stepped back thirty-five years. And I stepped out of it – alive – nine days before the fire!"

He looked again at Roger.

"What about him?" he wondered. "He isn't thirty years old. So he wasn't alive at the time of the fire. *But I saw him in the hotel – before the fire*. Is he a man from another time? Is he a man from yesterday?"

Sam remembered the girl's words: "*Nobody knows much about him. He's a strange man.*"

"And what about his 'holiday' every year in February?" Sam thought. "Does he go back to 1947 every year in February? Why? Maybe he *has* to go back. Maybe he has never really escaped from the past. But why? Why hasn't he escaped from the past?"

Then Sam remembered another thing.

Roger came back with Sam's coffee on a tray.

"You've been a very good waiter," Sam said. "I want to give you something, Roger." He gave the waiter a packet of cigarettes. "Here you are, Roger," he said. "A packet of cigarettes for you."

Roger dropped the tray, and it crashed to the floor.

"I – I – don't smoke," he said, and he moved away from Sam. He did not take his eyes from the cigarettes. "*I don't smoke now*," he shouted. "*Do you hear me? I don't smoke now!*"

And he ran from the room.

Sam never stayed at the Woodlands Hotel again. He did not want to step back into the past again. "Maybe, like Roger, I won't escape next time," he thought.

Exercises

Double fear

pages

1–3
- *Why* did Greg go up Hangar Hill? (*Answer*: Because ...)
- *Where* did he first meet the Double?
- *Who* did not believe stories about UFOs?
- *What* is a UFO?

4–6
- *Why* did Mr Mason say, "Don't tell lies"? (*Answer*: Because ...)
- *Where* did Mike see the Double?
- *Who* always played snooker on Fridays? (Two people)
- *What* did Greg see through the club window?

9–10
- *Why* did the college head go into the ambulance?
- *Where* was the police car?
- *Who* started the fire at the college? (Two people)
- *What* did the Double do in Kimble Street?

12–14
- *Why* did the motorbike crash?
- *Where* did Greg meet his Double?
- *Who* had to make a "Transfer"? (Five people)
- *What* was in the Double's pocket?

15–18
- *Why* did David Blake die?
- *Where* did Greg and Mike first see Bill Harper?
- *Who* went to Mrs Harris's shop? (Two people)
- *What* book did Mike buy?

18–21
- *Why* did Mike go behind some bushes?
- *Where* did Bill Harper go?
- *Who* shouted to Bill Harper? (Five people)
- *What* did the policeman shout from the boat?

21–24
- *Why* did Bill Harper's double die?
- *Where* did Greg's double say, "I will know today"?
- *Who* phoned the police, and *who* phoned Greg's mother?
- *What* did Greg's double do in the end?

Did you understand the story?

   a The five doubles came from ...

   b They had to make the "Transfer" with: 1 Greg Mason. 2 ... 3 ... 4 and 5 ...

   c Only ... of the doubles did not die.

   d Why did the other doubles die?
  - 1 ....: Because he didn't know about motorbikes on ....
  - 2 ....: Because ....
  - 3 and 4 ....: Because they ....

   e In the end, Greg's double made the Transfer with .....

   f Why did he not make the Transfer with Greg?